DISCOVE MARTHA'S VINEYARD

A Comprehensive Travel Guide to All the Island has to Offer

JOSEPH L. PERALEZ

INTRODU CTION

A brief history of Martha's Vineyard

Martha's Vineyard is an island off the coast of Massachusetts, located south of Cape Cod. It has a rich and fascinating history, dating back thousands of years to its first inhabitants. Today, it is a popular vacation destination, known for its beautiful beaches, quaint towns, and rich culture. In this article, we will explore the history of Martha's Vineyard, from its early days to the present. The Wampanoag people were the first to call Martha's Vineyard home. They lived on the island for thousands of years, fishing and hunting for food, and cultivating crops. The Wampanoag were skilled boat builders and fishermen, and they had a close relationship with the sea. They used the island's abundant resources to create a vibrant and self-sustaining community.

In 1602, the English explorer Bartholomew Gosnold arrived on the island and named it Martha's Vineyard after his daughter and the wild grapes that grew there. Over the next few centuries, Martha's Vineyard became a center of the whaling industry. Whaling ships from all over the world sailed to the island to stock up on supplies and recruit crew members. The whaling industry brought wealth and prosperity to the island, and many residents became wealthy whaling captains.

However, the whaling industry also had a dark side. Whaling was a dangerous and brutal profession, and many sailors died or were injured in pursuit of the whales. The whaling ships also brought diseases to the island, which had devastating effects on the Wampanoag population. By the early 1800s, the Wampanoag people had been almost completely wiped out by disease and other factors. In the 1800s, Martha's Vineyard became a popular vacation destination for wealthy families from the Northeast. They built elaborate summer homes on the island, many of which still stand today. The island's natural beauty, with its rolling hills and pristine beaches, drew visitors from all over the world. The island also became known for its agricultural products, such as cranberries and oysters.

During World War II, Martha's Vineyard played an important role in the war effort. The island was used as a training ground for soldiers and sailors, and many military installations were built there. After the war, the island's economy shifted away from agriculture and towards tourism. Today, Martha's Vineyard is one of the most popular vacation destinations in the United States, attracting millions of visitors each year. In recent years, Martha's Vineyard has faced a number of challenges. Climate change has caused sea levels to rise, which has led to increased erosion and flooding on the island. In addition, the island's housing market has become increasingly expensive, making it difficult for many residents to afford to live there. However, the island's residents remain committed to preserving its natural beauty and rich culture.

Martha's Vineyard has a rich and complex history that spans thousands of years. From its first inhabitants, the Wampanoag people, to its current status as a popular vacation destination, the island has seen many changes over the years. Despite the challenges it faces, Martha's Vineyard remains a unique and special place, with a rich cultural heritage and a deep connection to the sea.

Overview of the island's geography and communities

Martha's Vineyard is a beautiful island rich in history and natural beauty, and it is made up of six distinct towns: Aquinnah, Chilmark, Edgartown, Oak Bluffs, Tisbury, and West Tisbury. Each town has its own unique character and charm, and together they make up one of the most popular vacation destinations in the United States.

Geography

Martha's Vineyard is roughly 100 square miles in size and has a year-round population of around 17,000 people. It is known for its rolling hills, pristine beaches, and lush forests. The island has a mild climate, with temperatures ranging from the mid-60s in the summer to the mid-30s in the winter. Martha's Vineyard is also home to a number of nature preserves, including the Manuel F. Correllus State Forest, which covers over 5,000 acres of land.

Communities

Aquinnah

Aquinnah, formerly known as Gay Head, is located on the western end of the island. It is home to the Wampanoag Indian Reservation, where members of the Wampanoag tribe live and work. The town is known for its stunning cliffs, which are made of vibrant red and orange clay. The Aquinnah Cliffs overlook the Atlantic Ocean and are a popular spot for hiking and sightseeing.

Chilmark

Chilmark is located on the southern end of the island and is known for its rolling hills and tranquil beaches. It is home to the Chilmark Community Center, which hosts a variety of events throughout the year, including concerts and lectures. Chilmark is also home to the Chilmark Chocolate Company, which makes handmade chocolates using locally sourced ingredients.

Edgartown

Edgartown is located on the eastern end of the island and is one of the island's most popular towns. It is known for its elegant homes and charming downtown area, which is filled with shops, restaurants, and galleries. Edgartown is also home to the Martha's Vineyard Museum, which houses a collection of artifacts and exhibits that tell the island's history.

Oak Bluffs

Oak Bluffs is located on the northeastern end of the island and is known for its colorful Victorian homes and lively downtown area. The town is home to the Flying Horses Carousel, which is the oldest operating carousel in the United States. Oak Bluffs is also home to the Martha's Vineyard Camp Meeting Association, which is a community of over 300 cottages that were built in the late 1800s.

Tisbury

Tisbury is located on the northwestern end of the island and is home to the main ferry terminal. The town is known for its Main Street, which is lined with shops, restaurants, and galleries. Tisbury is also home to the Vineyard Haven Harbor, which is a popular spot for boating and fishing.

West Tisbury

West Tisbury is located in the center of the island and is known for its farms and rural landscapes. The town is home to the West Tisbury Farmers' Market, which is held every Wednesday and Saturday and features locally grown produce, crafts, and other goods. West Tisbury is also home to the Polly Hill Arboretum, which is a 70-acre botanical garden that features a variety of plant species.

Martha's Vineyard is a beautiful and diverse island that is made up of six unique towns. Each town has its own distinct character and charm, and together they make up one of the most popular vacation destinations in the United States.

CHAPTER ONE

Exploring the Island

Martha's Vineyard is a beautiful island known for its picturesque towns, stunning beaches, and lush landscapes. With so much to see and do, exploring the island can be an adventure in itself. Whether you're interested in hiking, cycling, shopping, or simply enjoying the natural beauty of the island, there is something for everyone on Martha's Vineyard.

Hiking and Nature

For those who enjoy hiking and exploring nature, Martha's Vineyard has many options to offer. The Manuel F. Correllus State Forest is a 5,100-acre forest that offers over 14 miles of trails for hiking and biking. The forest is also home to a number of ponds, which are great for fishing and swimming. The Waskosim's Rock Reservation is another popular hiking spot on the island. It offers a scenic overlook of the Vineyard Sound and a variety of hiking trails that wind through the woods. For those interested in bird watching, Felix Neck Wildlife Sanctuary is a must-visit destination. It covers over 194 acres of land and offers a variety of habitats, including woodlands, meadows, ponds, and salt marshes. It is home to over 250 species of birds, making it a popular destination for birdwatchers.

Beaches

Martha's Vineyard is known for its stunning beaches, each with its own unique character and charm. South Beach is a popular destination for those looking to surf, swim, or sunbathe. The beach stretches for over 3 miles and offers a variety of activities, including volleyball, fishing, and boating. Menemsha Beach is another popular destination, known for its stunning sunsets and tranquil waters. It is also home to a number of seafood restaurants, making it a great spot for a seafood lunch or dinner.

Menemsha Beach

Cycling

Cycling is a popular way to explore Martha's Vineyard, with many of the island's roads offering scenic views of the coast and countryside. The State Forest offers a number of trails for cycling, as does the Martha's Vineyard Land Bank, which preserves over 3,100 acres of land on the island. The bike path that runs from Oak Bluffs to Edgartown is another popular cycling route, offering stunning views of the ocean and the town's beautiful architecture.

Shopping

Martha's Vineyard has a variety of shopping options, from quaint boutiques to upscale galleries. The town of Edgartown is home to a variety of high-end shops, offering everything from designer clothing to fine jewelry. The town of Vineyard Haven also offers a variety of shopping options, including bookstores, clothing stores, and art galleries. The Chilmark Flea Market is another popular destination for those looking for unique handmade crafts and gifts.

Dining

Martha's Vineyard is known for its fresh seafood and farm-to-table cuisine. The island is home to a variety of restaurants, from upscale eateries to casual seafood shacks. The Black Dog Tavern in Vineyard Haven is a popular destination for those looking for fresh seafood and stunning ocean views. The Beach Plum Inn in Chilmark offers farm-to-table cuisine made with ingredients sourced from local farms. Martha's Vineyard offers a variety of activities and destinations for those looking to explore the island. Whether you're interested in hiking, cycling, shopping, or simply enjoying the natural beauty of the island, there is something for everyone on Martha's Vineyard. With its stunning beaches, beautiful landscapes, and charming towns, it's no wonder that Martha's Vineyard is one of the most popular vacation destinations in the United States.

Beaches and coastal walks

Martha's Vineyard is an island off the coast of Massachusetts that is known for its stunning beaches and coastal walks. The island has over 120 miles of coastline, which means that there are plenty of options for visitors who want to enjoy the sun, sand, and surf. Here are some of the best beaches and coastal walks on Martha's Vineyard.

Beaches

South Beach - South Beach is one of the most popular beaches on Martha's Vineyard, and for good reason. This three-mile-long beach is perfect for swimming, sunbathing, and surfing. It's also a great spot for beach volleyball and fishing. South Beach has a large parking lot, and there are restrooms and showers available.

Oak Bluffs Town Beach - The Oak Bluffs Town Beach is a smaller beach that is perfect for families with young children. The beach has gentle waves and shallow water, which makes it a great spot for kids to swim. There is a playground on the beach, as well as restrooms and showers.

Aquinnah Public Beach - The Aquinnah Public Beach is located on the western end of the island and is known for its stunning views of the Gay Head Cliffs. The beach has gentle waves and is a great spot for swimming and sunbathing. There is a snack bar on the beach, as well as restrooms and showers.

State Beach - State Beach is a two-mile-long beach that is located between Edgartown and Oak Bluffs. The beach is popular with families, as it has gentle waves and shallow water. State Beach has a large parking lot, and there are restrooms and showers also available.

Coastal Walks

Menemsha Beach to Aquinnah Cliffs - The walk from Menemsha Beach to the Aquinnah Cliffs is a must-do for visitors to Martha's Vineyard. The walk takes you along the shoreline and offers stunning views of the ocean and the cliffs. The walk is approximately three miles long and takes about an hour to complete.

Katama Beach - The Katama Beach area is known for its beautiful dunes and grassy plains. The area has a number of walking trails that take visitors through the dunes and along the beach. The walking trails range in length from one to three miles.

Chappaquiddick Island - Chappaquiddick Island is located just off the eastern end of Martha's Vineyard and is accessible by ferry. The island has a number of walking trails that take visitors through the island's forests, fields, and along the coastline. The Mytoi Garden on Chappaquiddick Island is a beautiful Japanese garden that is also worth a visit.

Gay Head Cliffs - The Gay Head Cliffs are a must-see attraction on Martha's Vineyard. The cliffs are made up of layers of colorful clay and are a stunning sight. Visitors can take a walk along the top of the cliffs and enjoy the stunning views of the ocean and the surrounding landscape.

Martha's Vineyard is home to some of the most beautiful beaches and coastal walks in the United States. Whether you want to spend the day swimming and sunbathing on the beach or taking a leisurely walk along the coastline, there are plenty of options available on the island. From South Beach to the Aquinnah Cliffs, there are plenty of stunning sights to see and activities to enjoy on Martha's Vineyard.

Hiking trails and nature preserves

Martha's Vineyard is a paradise for nature lovers, with its miles of pristine beaches, serene forests, and rolling hills. The island is home to numerous hiking trails and nature preserves that offer visitors a chance to explore the island's natural beauty and wildlife. Here are some of the best hiking trails and nature preserves on Martha's Vineyard.

Hiking Trails

Manuel F. Correllus State Forest - The Manuel F. Correllus State Forest is a 5,000-acre forest located in the center of Martha's Vineyard. The forest has over 14 miles of hiking trails that wind through oak and pine forests and offer stunning views of the island's landscape. The trails vary in difficulty, from easy to moderate, and are open year-round.

Waskosim's Rock Reservation - The Waskosim's Rock Reservation is a 25-acre nature reserve located in West Tisbury. The reserve has two trails that wind through hardwood forests and offer stunning views of the island's landscape. The trails are relatively short, with the longest being just over a mile, but they offer visitors a chance to see the island's wildlife up close.

Long Point Wildlife Refuge - The Long Point Wildlife Refuge is a 600-acre nature preserve located on the southern end of Martha's Vineyard. The preserve has over four miles of hiking trails that wind through salt marshes, sand dunes, and beach grass fields. The trails offer stunning views of the ocean and are home to a variety of wildlife, including deer, foxes, and ospreys.

Nature Preserves

Felix Neck Wildlife Sanctuary - The Felix Neck Wildlife Sanctuary is a 194-acre nature preserve located in Edgartown. The sanctuary has several trails that wind through salt marshes, hardwood forests, and meadows. Visitors can also explore the sanctuary's nature center, which has exhibits on the island's wildlife and natural history.

Mytoi Garden - The Mytoi Garden is a beautiful Japanese garden located on Chappaquiddick Island. The garden has a series of paths that wind through the garden's ponds, bridges, and stone lanterns. Visitors can also explore the garden's forests and fields, which are home to a variety of wildlife, including turtles and frogs.

Chilmark Pond Preserve - The Chilmark Pond Preserve is a 40-acre nature preserve located in Chilmark. The preserve has several trails that wind through oak and pine forests and offer stunning views of Chilmark Pond. The trails are relatively short, with the longest being just over a mile, but they offer visitors a chance to see the island's wildlife up close.

Martha's Vineyard is a nature lover's paradise, with its miles of pristine beaches, serene forests, and rolling hills. The island's hiking trails and nature preserves offer visitors a chance to explore the island's natural beauty and wildlife up close. Whether you want to hike through the Manuel F. Correllus State Forest or explore the Felix Neck Wildlife Sanctuary, there are plenty of options available for visitors who want to experience the island's natural wonders.

Towns and villages to visit

Martha's Vineyard is an island known for its quaint towns, picturesque villages, and charming neighborhoods. Each town on the island has its unique charm and character, making it a great place to explore for visitors. Here are some of the best towns and villages to visit on Martha's Vineyard.

Edgartown - Edgartown is the largest town on Martha's Vineyard and has a rich history dating back to the 17th century. The town's architecture is stunning, with many historic homes and buildings still standing today. Visitors can explore the town's cobblestone streets and visit landmarks such as the Old Whaling Church and the Edgartown Lighthouse. The town is also home to numerous boutiques, galleries, and restaurants.

Oak Bluffs - Oak Bluffs is a quaint town on the northeast coast of Martha's Vineyard. The town is known for its charming gingerbread houses, which are brightly colored Victorian-style homes with ornate trim and decorative features. Visitors can stroll through the town's streets and admire the unique architecture or take a ride on the Flying Horses Carousel, one of the oldest operating carousels in the country. Oak Bluffs is also home to several beaches, parks, and restaurants.

Vineyard Haven - Vineyard Haven is a bustling port town on the north coast of Martha's Vineyard. The town is known for its vibrant arts scene, with numerous galleries, theaters, and cultural institutions. Visitors can explore the town's shops and restaurants, stroll along the waterfront, or visit landmarks such as the Martha's Vineyard Playhouse or the historic Vineyard Haven Public Library.

Chilmark - Chilmark is a quiet and rural town on the western coast of Martha's Vineyard. The town is known for its stunning natural beauty, with rolling hills, pristine beaches, and picturesque farmland. Visitors can explore the town's beaches, parks, and trails or visit landmarks such as the Chilmark Tavern or the Chilmark Community Center.

West Tisbury - West Tisbury is a charming village located in the center of Martha's Vineyard. The village is known for its rural character, with numerous farms, fields, and woodlands. Visitors can explore the village's shops and restaurants, stroll through the town's parks and trails, or visit landmarks such as the West Tisbury Library or the Field Gallery.

Aquinnah - Aquinnah is a small town located on the westernmost point of Martha's Vineyard. The town is known for its stunning cliffs and beaches, including the famous Gay Head Cliffs. Visitors can explore the town's beaches, parks, and trails or visit landmarks such as the Aquinnah Lighthouse or the Martha's Vineyard Museum.

Martha's Vineyard is a charming island with numerous towns and villages to explore. From the historic streets of Edgartown to the quaint gingerbread houses of Oak Bluffs, each town on the island has its unique charm and character. Whether you want to soak up the island's rich history or explore its stunning natural beauty, there is something for everyone on Martha's Vineyard.

Vineyard tours and activities

Martha's Vineyard is a popular destination for travelers looking for a relaxing and enjoyable vacation. One of the best ways to experience the island's charm and beauty is by taking a vineyard tour or participating in other activities. Here are some of the top vineyard tours and activities to consider during your visit to Martha's Vineyard.

Vineyard Tours:

Martha's Vineyard Wine Tours - Martha's Vineyard Wine Tours is one of the top vineyard tour companies on the island. They offer a range of tours that take visitors to some of the island's top wineries, including the award-winning Chilmark Winery and the charming West Tisbury Farmer's Market. The tours also include a knowledgeable guide who will share information about the island's history, culture, and wine-making traditions.

Sharky's Vineyard Tour - Sharky's Vineyard Tour is a unique and entertaining way to explore the island's vineyards. Visitors hop on a vintage bus that has been converted into a mobile wine-tasting room, complete with comfortable seating and a sound system. The tour stops at several vineyards and wineries, including the picturesque Martha's Vineyard, where visitors can enjoy tastings and take in the stunning views of the surrounding countryside.

Edgartown Trolley Tour - For those looking to explore the island's history and culture, the Edgartown Trolley Tour is a great option. The tour takes visitors on a leisurely ride through Edgartown's historic district, where they can see some of the town's most beautiful homes and landmarks. The tour includes a knowledgeable guide who will share stories and insights about the town's rich history and culture.

Activities:

Bike Tours - Martha's Vineyard is a great place to explore on a bike, with miles of scenic bike paths and quiet roads. Several tour companies offer guided bike tours that take visitors to some of the island's top sights, including beaches, lighthouses, and vineyards. Some tours even include tastings at local vineyards, making for a fun and memorable experience.

Kayaking - Kayaking is a popular activity on Martha's Vineyard, with several companies offering guided tours and rentals. Visitors can explore the island's beautiful coastline and waterways, taking in the stunning scenery and spotting wildlife such as seals and ospreys. Some tours even include stops at secluded beaches or islands, where visitors can enjoy a picnic lunch or a swim in the clear, blue water.

Fishing Charters - Martha's Vineyard is known for its excellent fishing opportunities, with abundant fish species such as striped bass, bluefish, and bonito. Several companies offer fishing charters that take visitors out to some of the island's top fishing spots, including the famous Martha's Vineyard Striped Bass and Bluefish Derby. The charters include an experienced guide who will provide equipment, bait, and tips on how to catch the big one.

Martha's Vineyard offers a range of vineyard tours and activities for visitors of all ages and interests. Whether you want to explore the island's natural beauty on a bike or kayak, or learn about its rich history and culture on a trolley tour, there is something for everyone on this charming island. So, plan your visit today and discover the best of Martha's Vineyard!

CHAPTER TWO

Dining and Nightlife

When it comes to dining and nightlife, Martha's Vineyard offers a diverse range of options to suit all tastes and preferences. From fresh seafood to farm-to-table cuisine, and from casual beachfront bars to elegant fine dining restaurants, there is something for everyone on this picturesque island. Here are some of the top dining and nightlife destinations to check out during your visit to Martha's Vineyard.

Dining:

The Black Dog Tavern - The Black Dog Tavern is one of the most iconic restaurants on Martha's Vineyard, offering delicious seafood and American fare in a cozy and inviting atmosphere. Located on the waterfront in Vineyard Haven, the restaurant has been serving visitors and locals for over 40 years. Some of the menu highlights include the lobster bisque, fish and chips, and the famous Black Dog burger.

State Road Restaurant - State Road Restaurant is a farm-to-table restaurant located in the charming town of West Tisbury. The restaurant offers a seasonal menu that features locally-sourced ingredients and creative dishes that are both sophisticated and approachable. Some of the menu highlights include the roasted beet salad, the grilled octopus, and the roasted chicken with polenta.

The Beach Plum Inn - The Beach Plum Inn is an elegant restaurant located in the town of Chilmark, offering breathtaking views of the surrounding countryside and the ocean. The restaurant offers a refined and upscale menu that highlights the best of New England cuisine, including fresh seafood and locally-grown produce. Some of the menu highlights include the seared scallops, the grilled swordfish, and the crispy duck confit.

Nightlife:

The Port Hunter - The Port Hunter is a lively and energetic bar and restaurant located in Edgartown. The bar features a wide selection of craft beers, cocktails, and wines, and the restaurant offers a menu of inventive and delicious small plates that are perfect for sharing. The atmosphere is casual and inviting, with live music and trivia nights adding to the fun.

The Ritz Cafe - The Ritz Cafe is a classic dive bar located in Oak Bluffs, offering cheap drinks and a fun and laid-back atmosphere. The bar features live music and karaoke nights, and the outdoor patio is the perfect place to relax and people-watch. The Ritz is a popular spot for locals and visitors alike, and is known for its fun and friendly vibe.

The Lampost - The Lampost is a popular bar and nightclub located in Oak Bluffs, featuring a spacious dance floor and a lineup of DJs and live music acts. The bar offers a wide selection of drinks and a fun and energetic atmosphere that is perfect for dancing and socializing. The Lampost is a popular destination for both locals and visitors, and is a great place to let loose and have some fun.

Martha's Vineyard offers a diverse range of dining and nightlife options for visitors to explore and enjoy. From casual beachfront bars to elegant fine dining restaurants, and from live music venues to nightclubs, there is something for everyone on this charming island. So, whether you are looking for a romantic dinner for two or a night out with friends, be sure to check out some of the top dining and nightlife destinations on Martha's Vineyard.

Local seafood and farm-to-table restaurants

Martha's Vineyard is well-known for its local seafood and farm-to-table restaurants. With its fertile farmlands and abundant coastline, the island offers a rich and diverse array of fresh and locally-sourced ingredients that inspire chefs and foodies alike. Here are some of the top local seafood and farm-to-table restaurants to check out during your visit to Martha's Vineyard.

Local Seafood:

The Net Result - The Net Result is a seafood market and restaurant located in Vineyard Haven, offering a variety of fresh seafood and prepared dishes to take away or enjoy on-site. The market offers a wide selection of fish and shellfish, including clams, oysters, scallops, lobster, and fish of all kinds. The restaurant features a menu of classic

New England seafood dishes, including fish and chips, lobster rolls, and clam chowder.

The Bite - The Bite is a casual seafood shack located in Menemsha, offering some of the best fried seafood on the island. The menu features a variety of classic New England dishes, including fish and chips, clam strips, and lobster rolls. The outdoor seating area overlooks the harbor and offers a stunning view of the sunset.

Larsen's Fish Market - Larsen's Fish Market is a family-owned and operated fish market and restaurant located in Menemsha, offering fresh and sustainably-sourced seafood to visitors and locals alike. The market offers a variety of fish and shellfish, including local scallops, lobsters, and clams. The restaurant features a menu of classic New England seafood dishes, including fish and chips, clam chowder, and lobster bisque.

Farm-to-Table Restaurants:

The Beach Plum Inn - The Beach Plum Inn, located in Chilmark, is a farm-to-table restaurant that offers breathtaking views of the surrounding countryside and the ocean. The restaurant's menu features seasonal and locally-sourced ingredients, including fresh seafood, meats, and vegetables. Some of the menu highlights include the seared scallops, the grilled swordfish, and the crispy duck confit.

State Road Restaurant - State Road Restaurant is a farm-to-table restaurant located in West Tisbury, offering a seasonal menu that highlights locally-sourced ingredients and creative dishes. The menu features a variety of small plates, entrees, and desserts that showcase the best of New England cuisine. Some of the menu highlights include the roasted beet salad, the grilled octopus, and the roasted chicken with polenta.

The Kitchen Porch - The Kitchen Porch is a cooking school and farm-to-table restaurant located in West Tisbury, offering a unique and immersive culinary experience for visitors. The restaurant's menu features a variety of creative and innovative dishes that highlight the best of Martha's Vineyard's seasonal ingredients. Some of the menu highlights include the roasted beet and goat cheese tart, the pan-seared cod with tomato and olive relish, and the flourless chocolate cake with whipped cream.

Martha's Vineyard offers a rich and diverse array of local seafood and farm-to-table restaurants that showcase the best of the island's natural bounty. Whether you are in the mood for classic New England seafood dishes or innovative and creative cuisine, there is something for everyone on this charming island. So, be sure to check out some of the top local seafood and farm-to-table restaurants during your visit to Martha's Vineyard and savor the flavors of this unique and beautiful destination.

Vineyard-made wines and beers

Martha's Vineyard has a burgeoning wine and beer scene that is becoming increasingly popular among visitors to the island. With a unique microclimate that allows for the growth of various types of grapes, as well as an abundance of local hops and grains, the island offers a rich and diverse array of vineyard-made wines and beers that are sure to delight any palate. Here are some of the top vineyard-made wines and beers to check out during your visit to Martha's Vineyard.

Wines:

Martha's Vineyard is home to several vineyards that produce exceptional wines, including Chilmark-based The Grey Barn and West Tisbury-based The Allen Farm. These vineyards grow grapes that are perfectly suited to the island's climate, resulting in wines that are both unique and delicious. Here are some of the top vineyard-made wines to try during your visit:

The Grey Barn - The Grey Barn is a family-owned and operated farm and vineyard located in Chilmark. The vineyard produces a variety of wines, including Chardonnay, Pinot Gris, Pinot Noir, and Cabernet Franc. The vineyard's wines are made using traditional methods, and are aged in French oak barrels, resulting in a complex and nuanced flavor profile.

The Allen Farm - The Allen Farm is a small, family-owned vineyard located in West Tisbury. The vineyard produces a variety of wines, including Chardonnay, Riesling, and Pinot Noir. The vineyard's wines are made using organic and sustainable farming methods, resulting in wines that are both delicious and environmentally friendly.

Beers:

Martha's Vineyard is also home to several craft breweries that produce exceptional beers using local hops and grains. These breweries offer a variety of beer styles, from traditional ales and lagers to more experimental brews. Here are some of the top vineyard-made beers to try during your visit:

Offshore Ale Company - The Offshore Ale Company is a brewpub located in Oak Bluffs that offers a variety of handcrafted beers and pub fare. The brewery's beers are made using locally-sourced hops and grains, and feature a variety of styles, including pale ales, stouts, and porters. Some of the brewery's top beers include the Island Light Lager, the Menemsha Creek Pale Ale, and the Hop Goddess Double IPA.

Bad Martha Beer - Bad Martha Beer is a craft brewery located in Edgartown that specializes in small-batch, artisanal beers. The brewery uses locally-sourced hops and grains, as well as other unique ingredients, to create a variety of delicious and distinctive beers. Some of the brewery's top beers include the Vineyard Summer Ale, the Chocolate Stout, and the Cranberry Sour.

Vineyard-owned wineries and breweries are also a popular destination for visitors to Martha's Vineyard, with many offering tours and tastings of their wines and beers. These tours provide a unique opportunity to learn about the winemaking and brewing process, as well as to sample some of the island's best wines and beers. Some of the top wineries and breweries to visit during your trip include The Grey Barn, The Allen Farm, Offshore Ale Company, and Bad Martha Beer.

Martha's Vineyard offers a rich and diverse array of vineyard-made wines and beers that are sure to delight any palate. Whether you are a fan of traditional wine and beer styles or more experimental brews, there is something for everyone on this charming island. So, be sure to check out some of the top vineyard-made wines and beers during your visit to Martha's Vineyard and savor the flavors of this unique and beautiful destination.

Live music and entertainment venues

Martha's Vineyard is home to a vibrant music and entertainment scene, with a variety of live music venues and events taking place throughout the island. From intimate coffeehouses to outdoor amphitheaters, there are plenty of opportunities to catch some great live music during your visit to the Vineyard. Here are some of the top music and entertainment venues to check out during your stay:

The Port Hunter - The Port Hunter is a popular restaurant and bar located in Edgartown that features live music performances several nights a week. The venue offers a variety of genres, including folk, rock, and blues, and is a great spot to grab a bite to eat and enjoy some live music.

The Ritz - The Ritz is a lively nightclub located in Oak Bluffs that features a variety of music genres, including hip hop, reggae, and EDM. The venue is open late and is a popular spot for dancing and socializing.

The Loft - The Loft is a cozy coffeehouse and performance venue located in Oak Bluffs that features a variety of live music performances throughout the year. The venue offers a relaxed and intimate atmosphere, making it a great spot to catch up-and-coming local artists.

Old Whaling Church - The Old Whaling Church is a historic church located in Edgartown that has been transformed into a performing arts center. The venue hosts a variety of events throughout the year, including concerts, theater performances, and dance recitals.

Vineyard Haven Bandstand - The Vineyard Haven Bandstand is an outdoor amphitheater located in Owen Park that hosts a variety of concerts and performances during the summer months. The venue offers stunning views of the harbor and is a great spot to enjoy some live music in a beautiful outdoor setting.

The Lampost - The Lampost is a popular bar and nightclub located in Oak Bluffs that features live music performances several nights a week. The venue offers a variety of genres, including rock, reggae, and hip hop, and is a great spot to grab a drink and enjoy some live music.

Island Theatre - The Island Theatre is a historic movie theater located in Oak Bluffs that also hosts live music performances and other events throughout the year. The venue offers a unique and intimate atmosphere and is a great spot to catch a concert or event.

In addition to these venues, there are also several annual music and entertainment events that take place on Martha's Vineyard. These include the Martha's Vineyard Jazz and Blues Summerfest, the Vineyard Artisans Festival, and the Martha's Vineyard International Film Festival. These events offer a great opportunity to experience the island's vibrant music and entertainment scene, as well as to meet other locals and visitors who share your interests.

Martha's Vineyard offers a rich and diverse music and entertainment scene that is sure to satisfy any music lover or culture enthusiast. With a variety of live music venues and events taking place throughout the island, there is always something happening on the Vineyard. So, be sure to check out some of the top music and entertainment venues during your stay and enjoy the vibrant and exciting culture of this beautiful island.

CHAPTER THREE

Accommodations

Martha's Vineyard offers a wide range of accommodation options for visitors to the island. Whether you're looking for a luxurious resort, a cozy bed and breakfast, or a family-friendly rental home, there are plenty of options to choose from. Here are some of the top accommodation options to consider during your stay:

Hotels and Resorts - Martha's Vineyard is home to several hotels and resorts that offer luxurious accommodations and a wide range of amenities. Some of the top options include The Harbor View Hotel in Edgartown, The Winnetu Oceanside Resort in Katama, and the Nobnocket Boutique Inn in Vineyard Haven. These properties offer everything from beach access and ocean views to spa services and fine dining.

Bed and Breakfasts - If you're looking for a more intimate and personalized experience, a bed and breakfast may be the perfect option for you. Martha's Vineyard has several bed and breakfasts that offer charming accommodations and a home-like atmosphere. Some of the top options include The Thorncroft Inn in Vineyard Haven, The Ashley Inn in Edgartown, and The Pequot Hotel in Oak Bluffs.

Rental Homes - For families or groups traveling together, a rental home may be the best option. There are many rental properties available on Martha's Vineyard, ranging from cozy cottages to spacious luxury homes. Some of the top rental companies include Sandpiper Rentals, Island Home Rentals, and Martha's Vineyard Vacation Rentals.

Martha's Vineyard Vacation Rentals.

Camping - For those who enjoy the great outdoors, there are several camping options on Martha's Vineyard. The most popular option is the Martha's Vineyard Family Campground, which offers tent and RV sites, as well as cabin rentals. The campground is located in Vineyard Haven and offers a range of amenities, including a swimming pool, playground, and camp store.

Inns and Guesthouses - In addition to bed and breakfasts, Martha's Vineyard also has several inns and guesthouses that offer charming accommodations and personalized service. Some of the top options include The Menemsha

Inn in Chilmark, The Summercamp Hotel in Oak Bluffs, and The Lambert's Cove Inn in West Tisbury.

The Summercamp Hotel

No matter which type of accommodation you choose, it's important to book in advance, especially during peak season (June through August). Many properties require a minimum stay of several nights, and rates can vary greatly depending on the time of year and the location. Some properties may also offer discounts or special packages, so be sure to do your research and compare options before booking.

Martha's Vineyard offers a variety of accommodation options to suit every traveler's needs and preferences. From luxurious hotels and resorts to cozy bed and breakfasts and rental homes, there are plenty of options to choose from. When planning your trip, be sure to consider your budget, location preferences, and desired amenities to find the perfect accommodation for your stay on this beautiful island.

Hotels and inns

Martha's Vineyard is known for its stunning scenery, quaint towns, and charming bed and breakfasts, but the island also boasts a variety of upscale hotels and inns that offer a luxurious stay for visitors. From historic properties with ocean views to modern resorts with top-notch amenities, there's a hotel or inn on Martha's Vineyard to suit every traveler's taste.

The Harbor View Hotel - Located in the heart of Edgartown, The Harbor View Hotel is one of the island's most iconic properties. The hotel dates back to 1891 and has been beautifully restored to its former glory, with elegant furnishings and stunning views of the harbor. The Harbor View offers a range of room types, from classic rooms to spacious suites, and features amenities like an outdoor pool, tennis courts, and a private beach.

The Winnetu Oceanside Resort - Situated on 11 acres in the Katama area of Edgartown, The Winnetu Oceanside Resort is a modern resort that offers a variety of accommodations, including hotel rooms, suites, and private cottages. The resort is located just steps from

South Beach, one of Martha's Vineyard's most beautiful beaches, and features amenities like a heated outdoor pool, tennis courts, and a fitness center.

The Charlotte Inn - Located in the heart of Edgartown, The Charlotte Inn is a luxurious property that offers a truly unique experience for guests. The inn is housed in three historic homes that date back to the 1800s and features 20 guest rooms that are elegantly decorated with antiques and fine art. The Charlotte Inn also features a private garden, a fine dining restaurant, and a spa.

The Nobnocket Boutique Inn - Located in the town of Vineyard Haven, The Nobnocket Boutique Inn is a small, luxury inn that offers a personalized experience for guests. The inn has just seven guest rooms, each decorated in a unique style and featuring amenities like luxury linens, Nespresso machines, and Molton Brown bath products. The Nobnocket also features a spa and a gourmet breakfast served each morning.

The Mansion House Inn - Situated in the heart of Vineyard Haven, The Mansion House Inn is a modern property that offers a range of accommodations, from standard rooms to spacious suites. The inn features amenities like an indoor pool, a fitness center, and a rooftop sundeck with views of the harbor. The Mansion House also has a spa and a restaurant that serves local seafood and other regional specialties.

The Beach Plum Inn - Located in the town of Chilmark, The Beach Plum Inn is a charming property that offers a peaceful retreat for guests. The inn has 15 guest rooms, each decorated in a classic New England style, and features amenities like a heated outdoor pool, a tennis court, and a farm-to-table restaurant. The Beach Plum Inn also offers panoramic views of the surrounding countryside and is just a short walk from Menemsha Beach.

Whether you're looking for a historic property with old-world charm or a modern resort with all the latest amenities, Martha's Vineyard has a range of hotels and inns to suit every traveler's needs. With stunning ocean views, beautiful gardens, and top-notch service, these properties offer a luxurious stay for visitors to the island. Be sure to book in advance, especially during peak season, to secure the best room at the best price.

Vacation rentals and Airbnb options

Martha's Vineyard is a popular vacation destination, and many visitors prefer the comfort and privacy of a vacation rental or Airbnb over a traditional hotel or inn. Fortunately, there are many options available on the island, from cozy cottages to spacious beachfront homes.

Vacation Rentals - There are many rental agencies on Martha's Vineyard that offer a range of properties to suit every need and budget. Some popular agencies include Point B Realty, Sandpiper Rentals, and Martha's Vineyard Vacation Rentals. These agencies offer properties all over the island, from the quaint towns of

Edgartown and Vineyard Haven to the secluded beaches of Chilmark and Aquinnah. Many vacation rentals on Martha's Vineyard offer amenities like fully equipped kitchens, outdoor grills, and private decks or patios. Some also offer beach access or even private beaches. Many rentals also come with linens and towels, so you don't have to worry about packing your own.

One advantage of renting a vacation home is that you have more space and privacy than you would in a hotel room. This can be particularly important for families or groups of friends traveling together. You also have the option to cook your own meals, which can save you money and be more convenient than eating out every day.

Airbnb - Airbnb has become a popular option for travelers to Martha's Vineyard in recent years. The site offers a range of properties, from spare rooms in private homes to entire houses or apartments. Many hosts on Airbnb are local residents who are happy to share their insider knowledge of the island with their guests.

One advantage of using Airbnb is that you can often find unique and quirky properties that you wouldn't find through a traditional rental agency. For example, you can rent a tiny house in the woods or a converted barn with ocean views. Another advantage is that Airbnb can often be more affordable than a hotel or vacation rental, especially if you're traveling on a budget. However, it's important to read reviews carefully and make sure you're renting from a reputable host.

When booking a vacation rental or Airbnb on Martha's Vineyard, it's important to book early, especially if you're traveling during peak season. Many properties book up quickly, and you don't want to miss out on your dream rental. It's also important to do your research and read reviews carefully before booking. Look for properties with good reviews and responsive hosts who are willing to answer your questions and address any concerns you may have. Overall, renting a vacation home or Airbnb on Martha's Vineyard can be a great way to experience the island like a local and enjoy all the comforts of home while on vacation. With so many options available, you're sure to find the perfect property to suit your needs and budget.

Camping and RV parks

For visitors looking to experience Martha's Vineyard's natural beauty in a more rustic way, camping and RV parks can be an ideal option. The island offers a variety of campgrounds and RV parks, each with its own unique features and amenities.

Camping - There are several campgrounds on Martha's Vineyard that offer tent camping. Some of the most popular include the Martha's Vineyard Family Campground, the Oak Bluffs Campground, and the Wampanoag Campground. These campgrounds offer sites for tents, as well as some sites for RVs. Tent camping is a great way to experience the island's natural beauty up close. Many campsites are nestled in wooded areas or near the island's picturesque ponds and lakes. Some campgrounds even offer ocean views. Many campsites offer fire pits and picnic tables, making it easy to enjoy a campfire or cook meals outdoors.

It's important to note that some campgrounds on Martha's Vineyard have restrictions on campfires or prohibit them altogether, so be sure to check before you go.

RV Parks - If you prefer the convenience and comfort of an RV, there are several parks on Martha's Vineyard that cater to RV travelers. These parks offer sites with full hookups, including water, electric, and sewer connections. Some of the most popular RV parks on the island include the Martha's Vineyard Family Campground, the Island Family Campground, and the Leisurewoods Oak Bluffs RV Park. These parks offer amenities like laundry facilities, showers, and even swimming pools. One thing to keep in mind is that RV parks on Martha's Vineyard can fill up quickly during peak season, so it's important to book your site in advance. It's also important to note that some RV parks have restrictions on the size of RVs they can accommodate, so be sure to check before you book.

While camping and RV parks may not offer the luxury amenities of a hotel or vacation rental, they can be a great way to experience Martha's Vineyard's natural beauty and save money on lodging. They also offer a unique sense of community, as campers often gather around campfires or share meals together.

When planning your camping or RV trip to Martha's Vineyard, it's important to pack appropriately for the season. The island can get chilly at night even in the summer, so be sure to bring warm layers and blankets. Bug spray is also a must-have, as the island is home to a variety of biting insects. Overall, camping and RV parks offer a unique way to experience Martha's Vineyard's natural beauty and can be a great option for travelers looking to save money on lodging. With a variety of options available, from tent camping to RV parks with full amenities, there's sure to be a camping or RV park that suits your needs and budget.

CHAPTER FOUR

Martha's Vineyard Culture

Martha's Vineyard has a unique and vibrant culture, shaped by its history, geography, and community. From its native Wampanoag roots to its thriving arts and culinary scenes, the island offers visitors a rich and diverse cultural experience.

Native Wampanoag Culture - Martha's Vineyard is home to the Wampanoag Tribe of Gay Head (Aquinnah), one of two federally recognized tribes in the state of Massachusetts. The Wampanoag people have inhabited the island for thousands of years and continue to maintain their cultural traditions and practices.

Wampanoag Homeland

Visitors can learn about Wampanoag culture at the Aquinnah Cultural Center, which features exhibits and educational programs on Wampanoag history, art, and language. The center also offers guided tours of Aquinnah's stunning cliffs and beaches, which hold great cultural significance for the tribe.

Arts and Culture - Martha's Vineyard has a thriving arts community, with galleries, museums, and cultural events showcasing local and regional artists. The Martha's Vineyard Museum in Vineyard Haven offers exhibits on the island's history, including its whaling and fishing industries, as well as rotating exhibits on local art and culture. The island is also home to several theaters, including the Martha's Vineyard Playhouse and the Island Theatre Workshop. These venues offer a variety of plays, musicals, and other performances throughout the year.

In addition to traditional arts, Martha's Vineyard is also known for its unique and eclectic fashion scene. The island's fashion designers and boutique shops offer a range of styles, from bohemian beachwear to elegant and timeless pieces.

Food and Culinary Traditions - Martha's Vineyard is a food lover's paradise, with a strong focus on local and sustainable cuisine. The island's farm-to-table movement is fueled by its fertile land and abundance of fresh seafood. Visitors can experience the island's culinary traditions at its many farm stands, which offer fresh produce, jams, and baked goods made from locally sourced ingredients. The island also boasts a number of award-winning restaurants, featuring inventive menus and locally caught seafood.

One culinary tradition unique to Martha's Vineyard is the "clambake," a traditional New England meal featuring clams, lobsters, and other seafood cooked in a pit on the beach. Visitors can experience a clambake at several locations on the island, including the Martha's Vineyard Clambake Company.

Community and Lifestyle - Martha's Vineyard has a strong sense of community, with a year-round population of about 16,000 residents. The island's tight-knit communities are made up of a diverse mix of people, including artists, farmers, fishermen, and business owners. The island's lifestyle is characterized by a laid-back, slower pace of life, with a focus on nature and outdoor activities. Many islanders enjoy boating, fishing, hiking, and other outdoor pursuits, as well as attending community events and festivals.

One event that showcases the island's unique culture and community spirit is the Martha's Vineyard Agricultural Fair, held every August. The fair features livestock exhibits, local crafts, and traditional games and competitions, such as pie-eating contests and tug-of-war.

In addition to the agricultural fair, the island hosts a variety of other cultural events throughout the year, including music festivals, art fairs, and film screenings. Overall, Martha's Vineyard's culture is defined by its rich history, strong community, and diverse range of artistic and culinary traditions. Whether you're interested in learning about the island's Native American roots, exploring its thriving arts scene, or experiencing its unique culinary traditions, there's something for everyone to discover on Martha's Vineyard.

Art galleries and museums

Martha's Vineyard is a hub of creativity, and it boasts several art galleries and museums. Whether you're an art aficionado or just appreciate beautiful things, the Vineyard's art scene is worth exploring.

The Granary Gallery in West Tisbury is one of the most popular galleries on the island. It showcases contemporary and traditional artwork, including paintings, sculptures, and photographs. The gallery is known for its expansive gardens, which feature several outdoor sculptures.

The Eisenhauer Gallery in Edgartown is another notable art space on the island. It showcases contemporary art, with a focus on works by emerging and mid-career artists. The gallery's collection includes paintings, sculptures, and mixed media pieces.

For those interested in African-American art, the Martha's Vineyard African-American Film Festival and Art Gallery is a must-visit. It showcases works by African-American artists, including paintings, photographs, and sculptures. In addition to the gallery, the festival also screens films by African-American filmmakers. The Vineyard Artisans Festivals, held twice a year, showcases works by local artists and artisans. Visitors can browse through a range of handcrafted items, including jewelry, pottery, textiles, and furniture. The festival provides a great opportunity to meet the artists and learn about their creative processes.

The Martha's Vineyard Museum in Vineyard Haven is a great place to learn about the island's history and culture. The museum features exhibits on the island's maritime heritage, Native American history, and agricultural past. Visitors can also explore the museum's extensive collection of historic photographs, maps, and artifacts.

The Polly Hill Arboretum in West Tisbury is another unique cultural attraction on the island. It showcases a vast collection of rare trees and shrubs from around the world. Visitors can take guided tours of the arboretum and learn about the plants' origins and unique features. The Martha's Vineyard Film Society screens movies year-round, including independent films, foreign films, and documentaries. The society also hosts special events and screenings, including the Martha's Vineyard International Film Festival.

For those interested in music, the Vineyard is home to several music festivals throughout the year. The Martha's Vineyard Jazz and Blues Summerfest, held in August, showcases local and national musicians performing jazz and blues music. The Martha's Vineyard Chamber Music Society also hosts concerts throughout the summer, featuring classical music performed by world-renowned musicians. Martha's Vineyard's art galleries and museums offer a unique and diverse cultural experience. From contemporary art to historic artifacts, there is something for everyone to explore and appreciate. Visitors can also attend music festivals, film screenings, and other cultural events to further immerse themselves in the island's vibrant arts scene.

Film and music festivals

Martha's Vineyard is home to several film and music festivals throughout the year, drawing visitors from all over the world who come to enjoy the island's unique cultural offerings. The Martha's Vineyard Film Festival is one of the most popular events on the island's cultural calendar. Held twice a year, the festival showcases a selection of independent and foreign films, as well as documentaries and shorts. The festival also includes panel discussions, Q&A sessions with filmmakers, and other special events.

Another popular film festival on the Vineyard is the Martha's Vineyard International Film Festival, which takes place in September. The festival showcases films from around the world, with a focus on promoting cultural understanding and dialogue. In addition to screenings, the festival also includes discussions with filmmakers, workshops, and other events. Music lovers will also find plenty to enjoy on the island, with several music festivals held throughout the year. The Martha's Vineyard Jazz and Blues Summerfest, held in August, features performances by local and national musicians, as well as workshops and other special events. The festival draws a diverse crowd, from jazz enthusiasts to families looking for a fun day out.

The Martha's Vineyard Chamber Music Society hosts a series of concerts throughout the summer, featuring performances by world-renowned musicians. The concerts take place in a variety of venues across the island, from churches to historic landmarks, and showcase a range of classical music styles. The Vineyard Sound, a popular a cappella group made up of college students, performs throughout the summer at various venues on the island. Their high-energy performances of contemporary hits and classic favorites draw large crowds and have become a beloved tradition on the Vineyard.

In addition to these larger festivals, there are also plenty of opportunities to enjoy live music throughout the year at local bars, restaurants, and cafes. Many venues feature a mix of local and touring musicians, playing everything from folk and blues to rock and jazz. The Vineyard also boasts a thriving theater scene, with several companies putting on performances throughout the year. The Martha's Vineyard Playhouse hosts a variety of productions, from classic plays to new works by emerging playwrights. The Island Theatre Workshop, a non-profit theater company, also puts on a variety of productions, including musicals, plays, and children's theater.

For those interested in comedy, the island is also home to several improv and sketch comedy troupes, such as The MV Improv Group and The Island Theatre Workshop's IMPers. These groups perform throughout the year, with shows that are both hilarious and thought-provoking. Martha's Vineyard's film and music festivals provide a unique and exciting way to experience the island's cultural scene. From independent films to world-renowned musicians, visitors can enjoy a diverse range of performances and events that showcase the best of what the Vineyard has to offer. Whether you're a film buff or a music lover, there is something for everyone to enjoy on this beautiful island.

Community events and traditions

Martha's Vineyard is known for its tight-knit community and unique traditions, which are celebrated throughout the year with a variety of events and festivals. From the annual agricultural fair to the Fourth of July parade, visitors to the island can experience the rich history and culture that make Martha's Vineyard so special. The Martha's Vineyard Agricultural Society hosts an annual fair every August, which has become a beloved tradition on the island. The fair features a variety of attractions, from carnival rides to agricultural displays and competitions. Visitors can sample local produce, watch animal shows, and enjoy live music and entertainment. The fair also includes a crafts fair, showcasing the work of local artisans.

Another popular event on the island is the annual Oak Bluffs fireworks display, held every Fourth of July. The fireworks are launched from the Oak Bluffs Harbor, with residents and visitors lining the shore to watch the spectacular show. The parade that precedes the fireworks is also a must-see event, featuring floats, marching bands, and community groups. The Chilmark Road Race is another beloved tradition on the Vineyard, with runners from all over the world coming to participate in this scenic 5K race. The race takes place on the Fourth of July, starting and ending at the Chilmark Community Center. The course winds through some of the island's most beautiful landscapes, including the rolling hills of Chilmark and the stunning ocean views along South Road.

For those who prefer a more laid-back atmosphere, the annual Pink and Green Weekend in Edgartown is a fun and festive event that celebrates the island's unique style and culture. The weekend includes a variety of activities, from shopping events to garden tours and cocktail parties. The highlight of the weekend is the Pink and Green Ball, where visitors can dance the night away in their best pink and green attire. The Martha's Vineyard Striped Bass and Bluefish Derby is another event that draws visitors from all over the world. Held every September, the derby is a fishing competition that rewards anglers for catching the biggest striped bass and bluefish. The derby also includes a variety of events, such as seminars and clinics on fishing techniques, as well as daily weigh-ins and awards ceremonies.

In addition to these larger events, there are also several community traditions that take place throughout the year. The Martha's Vineyard Playhouse hosts an annual Christmas Carol Sing-Along, where visitors can join in singing classic holiday songs. The Chilmark Potluck Jam, held every Wednesday in the summer, is a beloved gathering of local musicians and visitors, where everyone brings a dish to share and enjoys an evening of music and community. Overall, Martha's Vineyard's community events and traditions provide a unique way to experience the island's rich culture and history. From the annual agricultural fair to the Fourth of July parade and the Chilmark Road Race, visitors can participate in activities that have been cherished by the island's residents for generations. These events showcase the warm and welcoming community that makes Martha's Vineyard such a special place to visit.

CHAPTER FIVE

Living on the Island

Living on Martha's Vineyard is a dream for many, with its beautiful scenery, tight-knit community, and unique island lifestyle. However, like any place, there are both benefits and challenges to living on the island year-round. One of the most significant benefits of living on Martha's Vineyard is the sense of community. Islanders are known for their warmth and friendliness, and many residents describe the island as feeling like a small town. This can be especially appealing for families or those looking for a close-knit community.

Another benefit of living on the island is the access to nature and outdoor activities. With miles of beautiful beaches, hiking trails, and nature preserves, there is never a shortage of things to do outside. Islanders also have access to a variety of water sports, such as kayaking, paddleboarding, and sailing. In terms of employment, the island has a thriving tourism industry, which provides many job opportunities for residents. There are also opportunities in other industries, such as healthcare, education, and government.

However, living on the island does come with some challenges. One of the biggest challenges is the high cost of living. The cost of housing on the island is significantly higher than on the mainland, and many other expenses, such as groceries and utilities, are also more expensive.

Another challenge is the limited access to certain amenities, such as healthcare and shopping. While there are excellent medical facilities on the island, residents may need to travel off the island for specialized care. Additionally, while there are many unique and charming shops on the island, residents may need to travel off the island for larger shopping trips.

Transportation can also be a challenge on the island, particularly during the summer months when traffic can be heavy. The island is only accessible by ferry or small plane, and transportation on the island itself can be limited, with few public transportation options. Despite these challenges, many residents find the benefits of living on the island far outweigh any drawbacks. The sense of community and access to nature are just two of the many reasons why people choose to call Martha's Vineyard home. The island's unique lifestyle, with its focus on community, nature, and sustainability, is something that many residents find incredibly rewarding.

Living on Martha's Vineyard also provides many opportunities for involvement in the community. There are numerous volunteer opportunities, such as working with local conservation organizations, helping out at the annual agricultural fair, or volunteering at the local library. Residents can also get involved in local government by attending town meetings and serving on local committees. Living on Martha's Vineyard is a unique and rewarding experience. While there are challenges associated with living on an island, such as the high cost of living and limited access to certain amenities, the benefits of living on the island are many. The sense of community, access to nature, and unique island lifestyle are just a few of the reasons why residents choose to call Martha's Vineyard home. For those who are drawn to the island's natural beauty and close-knit community, living on Martha's Vineyard can be a truly fulfilling experience.

Real estate and housing options

Martha's Vineyard is a beautiful and unique place to live, and many people dream of owning a home on the island. However, the high demand and limited supply of real estate on the island can make finding the right property a challenge. One of the most significant factors that affect real estate on Martha's Vineyard is its limited land availability. With only about 100 square miles of land, the island has a finite amount of space for development. As a result, properties on the island tend to be more expensive than those on the mainland, with high demand driving up prices even further.

Housing options on the island are diverse, ranging from historic homes and quaint cottages to modern luxury estates. Many homes on the island are built in a traditional New England style, with features like shingled exteriors, white trim, and charming porches. For those looking to purchase property on the island, working with a local real estate agent is key. Local agents have a deep understanding of the island's real estate market and can help prospective buyers navigate the unique challenges of purchasing property on an island.

One popular housing option on the island is single-family homes. Many of these homes are historic properties, with some dating back to the 18th century. These homes offer a unique opportunity to own a piece of the island's history, with charming features like wide plank flooring, exposed beams, and wood-burning fireplaces. For those looking for a more low-maintenance option, condos and townhouses are also available on the island. These properties often offer amenities like swimming pools, fitness centers, and maintenance services, making them a great choice for those looking for a more hands-off approach to homeownership.

Another popular housing option on the island is vacation rentals. Many property owners choose to rent out their homes during the summer months, providing a steady stream of income and the flexibility to use the property themselves during the offseason. However, the rental market on Martha's Vineyard can be competitive, with high demand driving up prices. It's essential to work with a reputable property management company to ensure that your rental property is well-maintained and marketed effectively.

For those looking to build their own home on the island, there are many options for custom home construction. Working with a local builder is key, as they will have a deep understanding of the unique challenges of building on the island, including zoning regulations, building codes, and environmental concerns. Finally, there are also options for those looking for affordable housing on the island. The island's housing market can be competitive, but there are programs and initiatives in place to help make housing more accessible to all residents.

One such initiative is the Martha's Vineyard Housing Trust, a nonprofit organization that helps to create affordable housing opportunities for island residents. The trust offers a variety of programs, including shared-equity homeownership, rental assistance, and down payment assistance. Real estate on Martha's Vineyard is a unique and challenging market, but there are many options available for those looking to own property on the island. Whether you're looking for a historic home, a low-maintenance condo, or a custom-built estate, working with a local agent is key to navigating the island's real estate market. And for those looking for affordable housing options, there are programs and initiatives in place to help make homeownership more accessible to all residents. With its natural beauty, tight-knit community, and unique island lifestyle, owning property on Martha's Vineyard can be a truly rewarding experience.

Schools and education

Martha's Vineyard has a unique and diverse educational system that is highly regarded in the region. The island offers a variety of options for students of all ages, including public schools, private schools, and homeschooling.

Public Schools:

The Martha's Vineyard Public Schools (MVPS) system is made up of six schools, serving students from pre-kindergarten through high school. The schools are located in four of the six towns on the island, with the high school located in the town of Oak Bluffs. The MVPS system prides itself on providing high-quality education to all students, and offers a wide range of academic programs, including advanced placement courses, vocational education, and special education.

Private Schools:

Martha's Vineyard also has a number of private schools, including the **Martha's Vineyard Regional High School**, which offers a rigorous academic program, as well as a number of extracurricular activities and sports teams.

Additionally, there are a number of private elementary and middle schools on the island, offering small class sizes and individualized attention.

Martha's Vineyard Regional High School

Homeschooling:

Homeschooling is also a popular option on Martha's Vineyard, with a number of families choosing to educate their children at home. Homeschooling families have access to a variety of resources, including support groups, co-ops, and online resources.

Higher Education:

For those seeking higher education, there are a number of options on the mainland, including Cape Cod Community

College, which has a campus in nearby Barnstable. Additionally, many students from Martha's Vineyard attend colleges and universities throughout the country. Overall, the education system on Martha's Vineyard is highly regarded and offers a wide range of options for students of all ages. The schools and educators are committed to providing high-quality education to all students, and the island's unique environment provides a wealth of opportunities for learning and exploration.

Healthcare and services

Martha's Vineyard has a strong healthcare system that serves the needs of the island's year-round residents, as well as its many visitors. The island has several medical centers and hospitals, as well as a range of other healthcare services.

Martha's Vineyard Hospital:

The island's primary medical center is Martha's Vineyard Hospital, which is located in the town of Oak Bluffs. The hospital provides a wide range of services, including emergency care, inpatient and outpatient care, diagnostic imaging, laboratory services, and rehabilitation services. The hospital also has a number of specialty clinics, including cardiology, gastroenterology, and dermatology.

Other Medical Centers:

In addition to Martha's Vineyard Hospital, there are several other medical centers on the island, including the Martha's Vineyard Community Health Center, which provides primary care services to the island's residents, and the Vineyard Nursing Association, which provides home healthcare services.

Specialty Services:

Martha's Vineyard also has a range of specialty healthcare services, including mental health services, substance abuse treatment, and hospice care. There are several private practices on the island offering therapy and counseling services, as well as a number of support groups and community resources for those struggling with addiction or other mental health issues.

Emergency Services:

The island's emergency services are provided by the Martha's Vineyard Emergency Services, which includes both ambulance and fire services. The emergency services are staffed by highly trained professionals who are dedicated to providing the highest level of care to island residents and visitors. Overall, the healthcare system on Martha's Vineyard is comprehensive and responsive to the needs of the island's residents and visitors. The medical centers and hospitals are staffed by highly qualified professionals who are committed to providing excellent care, and the island's many specialty services provide a range of options for those with specialized healthcare needs. Additionally, the emergency services on the island are well-equipped to handle any situation that may arise, ensuring the safety and well-being of all who live and visit the island.

CHAPTER SIX

Getting Around

Martha's Vineyard is a relatively small island, but there are several options for getting around. Visitors have the choice of using public transportation, renting a car or bike, or taking advantage of ride-sharing services.

Public Transportation:

Martha's Vineyard has a public transportation system that is operated by the Martha's Vineyard Transit Authority (VTA). The VTA provides year-round bus service to all six towns on the island. During the summer months, the VTA offers extended hours and additional routes to accommodate the higher number of visitors. The buses are clean, safe, and air-conditioned, making them a popular option for tourists who want to explore the island without worrying about parking or traffic.

Rental Cars and Bikes:

Visitors to Martha's Vineyard can also rent a car or bike to get around the island. Several car rental companies have locations on the island, including Avis and Budget, and there are several bike rental shops as well. Renting a car or bike is a great option for those who want the freedom to explore the island at their own pace. However, it's important to note that traffic can be heavy during the summer months, so it's best to plan ahead and avoid peak travel times.

Ride-Sharing Services:

For those who prefer the convenience of ride-sharing services, companies like Uber and Lyft are available on the island. While these services are typically more expensive than public transportation or renting a car, they can be a good option for those who want to avoid driving or navigating public transportation.

Walking:

Walking is also a popular way to get around Martha's Vineyard, particularly in the towns of Edgartown and Oak Bluffs. These towns are relatively small and easy to navigate on foot, and visitors can enjoy the scenic beauty of the island while getting some exercise.

Ferry Services:

Finally, it's important to note that the only way to get to Martha's Vineyard is by ferry. Visitors can take a ferry from several locations on the mainland, including Woods Hole, Falmouth, and Hyannis. The ferry ride is a scenic experience in itself, and visitors can enjoy views of the ocean and the surrounding islands. There are several options for getting around Martha's Vineyard, including public transportation, rental cars and bikes, ride-sharing services, and walking. Visitors should choose the option that best suits their needs and preferences, keeping in mind that traffic can be heavy during the summer months. Regardless of how visitors choose to get around, the beauty and charm of Martha's Vineyard make every journey a memorable one.

Ferries and transportation to the island

Martha's Vineyard is an island located off the coast of Massachusetts, making ferry transportation the only way to reach the island by car or public transportation. There are several ferry services that offer transportation to Martha's Vineyard from different locations on the mainland.

The Steamship Authority:

The Steamship Authority is the most popular ferry service to Martha's Vineyard. It offers year-round ferry service from the mainland port of Woods Hole, which is located in Falmouth, Massachusetts. The ferry ride takes approximately 45 minutes to an hour, depending on the vessel used and the time of year. During the summer months, the Steamship Authority offers additional ferry routes and schedules to accommodate the higher number of visitors to the island.

Island Queen:

The Island Queen ferry service offers seasonal ferry transportation from the mainland port of Falmouth, Massachusetts. This ferry service offers a faster ride than the Steamship Authority, with the trip taking approximately 35 minutes. The Island Queen operates from Memorial Day weekend through Columbus Day.

Falmouth-Edgartown Ferry:

The Falmouth-Edgartown Ferry offers seasonal ferry service from the mainland port of Falmouth, Massachusetts to Edgartown on Martha's Vineyard. The ferry ride takes approximately 90 minutes, and it operates from Memorial Day weekend through Labor Day.

Hy-Line Cruises:

Hy-Line Cruises offers seasonal ferry service from Hyannis, Massachusetts, to Oak Bluffs on Martha's Vineyard. The ferry ride takes approximately 55 minutes, and it operates from Memorial Day weekend through

Columbus Day. Hy-Line Cruises also offers high-speed ferry service, which takes only 35 minutes.

Getting Around on the Island:

Once visitors arrive on Martha's Vineyard, there are several options for getting around the island. The Martha's Vineyard Transit Authority (VTA) provides year-round bus service to all six towns on the island. During the summer months, the VTA offers extended hours and additional routes to accommodate the higher number of visitors. Visitors can also rent a car or bike to get around the island, or use ride-sharing services like Uber and Lyft. Walking is also a popular way to explore the island, particularly in the towns of Edgartown and Oak Bluffs.

Ferries are the only way to reach Martha's Vineyard from the mainland, with several ferry services offering transportation to the island from different ports. Once on the island, visitors have several options for getting around, including public transportation, rental cars and bikes, ride-sharing services, and walking. Regardless of how visitors choose to get around, the scenic beauty and charm of Martha's Vineyard make every journey a memorable one.

Biking and public transportation

Martha's Vineyard is a great place to explore by bike or using public transportation. There are many bike rental shops available on the island, and the public transportation system, the Vineyard Transit Authority (VTA), offers bus services throughout the island. Here are some tips for getting around Martha's Vineyard by bike or public transportation.

Biking on Martha's Vineyard

Biking is a popular way to explore Martha's Vineyard. With miles of bike paths and quiet country roads, it's a great way to get around and see the island's natural beauty. There are several bike rental shops on the island that offer a variety of bikes for rent, including road bikes, mountain bikes, and beach cruisers. Many shops also provide helmets and maps of the island's bike paths. The Martha's Vineyard bike path system is made up of several different paths that connect many of the island's towns and beaches. The most popular path is the Vineyard Haven to Oak Bluffs path, which is just under four miles long and passes through several parks and beaches. Another popular path is the State Beach path, which runs from Oak Bluffs to Edgartown and provides stunning views of the ocean.

Biking on Martha's Vineyard is a great way to get exercise and explore the island's natural beauty. However, it's important to remember that some of the island's roads can be narrow and winding, so it's important to use caution and follow traffic laws.

Public Transportation on Martha's Vineyard

The Vineyard Transit Authority (VTA) provides bus services throughout Martha's Vineyard. The VTA operates several different bus routes that connect the island's towns and beaches, making it easy to get around without a car. The VTA also offers special event services for events like the Agricultural Fair and the Martha's Vineyard Film Festival. The VTA's bus routes operate from early morning until late at night, making it easy to get around the island at any time of day. Fares are reasonable, with discounts available for seniors and children.

In addition to the VTA, there are several other public transportation options available on Martha's Vineyard. Taxis and ride-sharing services are available, as well as private shuttle services that provide transportation to and from the island's major airports.

Tips for Getting Around Martha's Vineyard

Whether you're biking or using public transportation, here are some tips to help you get around Martha's Vineyard:

Plan ahead: Check the VTA's bus schedules and bike paths ahead of time to plan your route and avoid any confusion or delays.

Bring a map: While many bike rental shops provide maps, it's always a good idea to bring your own map or download a map of the island onto your phone.

Be aware of traffic: Some of the island's roads can be narrow and winding, so it's important to use caution and follow traffic laws. Stay to the right of the road and use hand signals to indicate turns.

Stay hydrated: Martha's Vineyard can get hot and humid during the summer months, so it's important to stay hydrated while biking or using public transportation. Bring a water bottle with you and refill it at one of the island's many public water fountains.

Be patient: While the VTA's bus system is reliable, it can be slow at times due to traffic and frequent stops. Be patient and enjoy the ride, and remember that you're on island time!

Biking and public transportation are great ways to explore Martha's Vineyard without a car. Whether you're looking to get some exercise or just want to relax and enjoy the island's natural beauty, there are plenty of options available to help you get around. Remember to plan ahead, bring a map, and stay safe while exploring all that

Car rentals and taxis

Martha's Vineyard is a beautiful island that can be best explored by car. The island offers a wide range of car rental services, including major brands like Hertz, Budget, and Enterprise, as well as local rental agencies. In addition, taxis are also available, making it easy for visitors to get around the island without having to worry about driving themselves. Car rentals are available in several locations across the island, including the Martha's Vineyard Airport, Oak Bluffs, Vineyard Haven, and Edgartown. Rates for car rentals typically vary depending on the season, with higher rates during peak summer months. Most rental agencies offer a range of vehicle types, from small economy cars to SUVs and minivans.

Taxis are another popular option for getting around the island. Visitors can easily hail a taxi on the street or call a local taxi company to arrange a pickup. Taxis are generally more expensive than renting a car, but they can be more convenient for those who prefer not to drive.

In addition to car rentals and taxis, Martha's Vineyard also offers public transportation options. The Martha's Vineyard Transit Authority operates a bus system that runs between major towns on the island, including Edgartown, Oak Bluffs, and Vineyard Haven. The buses are equipped with bike racks, making it easy for visitors to bring their bikes along for the ride.

For those who prefer a more active way of getting around the island, biking is a popular option. Martha's Vineyard has several bike rental shops, making it easy for visitors to rent bikes and explore the island's many bike paths and scenic routes. Biking is a great way to get some exercise and take in the island's natural beauty. Another option for getting around the island is by foot. Many of the island's towns and villages are easily walkable, and there are several walking tours available that allow visitors to explore the island's history and culture on foot.

Overall, getting around Martha's Vineyard is easy and convenient. With a variety of transportation options available, visitors can choose the method that best suits their needs and preferences. Whether by car, taxi, bus, bike, or foot, exploring the island is an enjoyable and unforgettable experience.

CONCLUSION

Tips for planning your trip to Martha's Vineyard

Martha's Vineyard is a wonderful destination that offers a variety of activities, attractions, and experiences. If you are planning a trip to the island, there are a few things to keep in mind to help you make the most of your time there.

Choose the right time to visit

Martha's Vineyard is a seasonal destination, with the busiest time being the summer months from June to September. During this time, the island can be quite crowded, and prices for accommodations and activities tend to be higher. If you prefer a quieter, more affordable visit, consider visiting in the spring or fall. The island is still beautiful during these times, and there are still plenty of activities and events to enjoy.

Book your accommodations early

Accommodations on Martha's Vineyard can be limited, particularly during the peak summer season. If you plan to visit during this time, it is recommended to book your accommodations early to ensure availability and avoid high prices. There are a variety of options for accommodations on the island, including hotels, inns, bed and breakfasts, vacation rentals, and campgrounds.

Plan your transportation in advance

Martha's Vineyard is an island, so getting there requires taking a ferry or plane. Ferries run regularly from the mainland, and it is recommended to make a reservation in advance, particularly during peak season. If you plan to bring a car to the island, be sure to book your reservation well in advance, as car space on the ferries can also be limited. Alternatively, you can rent a car or take a taxi once you arrive on the island.

Pack for the weather

The weather on Martha's Vineyard can be unpredictable, particularly in the spring and fall. It is recommended to pack layers and rain gear to be prepared for any weather conditions. In the summer, the weather is generally warm and sunny, so be sure to pack sunscreen and beach gear if you plan to spend time on the beaches.

Research activities and events in advance

There are many activities and events on Martha's Vineyard, so it is recommended to research and plan your itinerary in advance. Some popular activities include visiting the beaches, hiking, biking, kayaking, and visiting the local shops and restaurants. There are also many events throughout the year, such as the Martha's Vineyard Food and Wine Festival and the Martha's Vineyard Agricultural Fair.

Respect the island's culture and traditions

Martha's Vineyard is a unique destination with a rich history and culture. It is important to respect the island's traditions and customs, particularly those related to the Wampanoag tribe, who have a long history on the island. Additionally, the island is known for its conservation efforts, so be sure to follow any posted rules or regulations related to protecting the environment.

Embrace the island's laid-back vibe

Martha's Vineyard has a relaxed, laid-back atmosphere that many visitors find refreshing. Take the time to slow down and enjoy the island's natural beauty and unique culture. Whether you spend your time exploring the beaches, hiking the trails, or simply relaxing with a book, Martha's Vineyard is the perfect destination to unwind and recharge.

Planning a trip to Martha's Vineyard can be a rewarding and memorable experience. By following these tips and taking the time to research and plan your itinerary, you can make the most of your time on the island and fully immerse yourself in its natural beauty and unique culture.

Reflections on the island's unique character and charm

Martha's Vineyard is a place that holds a special place in the hearts of many. The island's unique character and charm have captivated visitors and residents alike for generations. From the picturesque beaches and charming towns to the lively cultural scene and friendly locals,

Martha's Vineyard is a destination that leaves a lasting impression.

One of the most striking things about Martha's Vineyard is the sense of community that permeates every aspect of life on the island. Despite its reputation as a vacation spot for the wealthy and famous, Martha's Vineyard remains a place where people from all walks of life come together to enjoy the island's natural beauty and vibrant culture.

Perhaps it is the island's isolation that has helped foster this strong sense of community. Located off the coast of Massachusetts, Martha's Vineyard can only be accessed by ferry or plane. This isolation has helped preserve the island's natural beauty and unique character, while also creating a close-knit community of residents and visitors.

One of the most beloved aspects of Martha's Vineyard is the abundance of natural beauty that can be found throughout the island. From the rolling hills and farmland in the up-island towns of Chilmark and West Tisbury to the sandy beaches and picturesque harbors in the down-island towns of Oak Bluffs and Edgartown, the island is a nature lover's paradise.

In addition to its natural beauty, Martha's Vineyard is also home to a thriving cultural scene. The island is home to a number of art galleries, museums, and performance venues, as well as several annual film and music festivals that draw visitors from all over the world.

Despite its many charms, however, Martha's Vineyard is not without its challenges. The island's isolation and limited resources can make life difficult for residents, particularly during the off-season when many businesses shut down and the population dwindles. Additionally, the island's popularity as a vacation destination can make it difficult to find affordable housing or to avoid crowds during peak tourist season.

Despite these challenges, however, the unique character and charm of Martha's Vineyard continue to draw visitors and residents to the island year after year. Whether you're looking to relax on the beach, explore the island's natural beauty, or immerse yourself in the local culture, there's something for everyone on Martha's Vineyard.

One of the most striking things about Martha's Vineyard is the way in which it balances tradition and modernity. While the island is home to a number of longstanding traditions and customs, it has also embraced change and innovation in many ways.

For example, Martha's Vineyard is home to a number of small businesses and startups, many of which are focused on sustainability and social responsibility. The island's agricultural heritage is also celebrated through a growing local food movement, which emphasizes farm-to-table dining and sustainable agriculture practices.

At the same time, Martha's Vineyard remains deeply connected to its history and traditions. The island's fishing industry, for example, has been a cornerstone of the local economy for generations, and continues to play an important role in the community today. Similarly, the island's many historic homes, churches, and landmarks are a testament to the rich history and cultural heritage of Martha's Vineyard.

Perhaps it is this balance of tradition and modernity that makes Martha's Vineyard such a special place. The island is home to a rich and diverse community of residents and visitors, all of whom share a deep appreciation for the island's natural beauty, cultural heritage, and sense of community.

In the end, it is this sense of community that truly sets Martha's Vineyard apart. Whether you're a long-time resident or a first-time visitor, there's a sense of camaraderie and mutual respect that pervades every aspect of life on the island.

Printed in Great Britain
by Amazon

25440287R00056